Introduction to Google Classroom

Annie Brock

KINGFISHER PRESS

To my favorite teacher, my mom.

Published in the United States by Kingfisher Press

Printed by: Createspace.com

10 9 8 7 6 5 4 3 2 1

Editor: Caety Klingman
Proofreader: Natalia Jaster
Cover design: Jake Flaherty

November 2015
New York, New York USA

Contents

PART I

The Google Classroom Advantage

As a twenty-first century teacher, you are facing a set of opportunities and challenges that no other teachers in the history of education have encountered. In the last ten years, an explosion of technology has radically changed the educational landscape. This technology has brought with it incredible benefits like more efficient communication, better access to knowledge and resources, and increased student engagement. But because of its relative newness, it's likely your pre-service teaching program did not adequately prepare you to effectively use technology as part of your teaching repertoire.

Today's teachers are poised to change both teaching and learning through integration of technology in the classroom. The business sector thrives on technology—in fact, many of the world's largest companies produce it, like Apple, Microsoft, and Google. The world has seen massive globalization thanks to the newfound ability to communicate instantaneously across the globe. Just as technology has transformed the way you live, it has the capacity to transform the way you teach. As the paradigm is shifting in other industries, so too in education are emerging technologies offering powerful alternatives to traditional methods. Despite these advancements, however, many of today's classrooms look virtually identical to the classrooms of fifty years ago.

Utilizing technology in new and interesting ways in the classroom isn't just important to keeping your teaching style fresh and relevant; it's essential experience for your students who will one day venture out to work and live in this technologically-driven world.

Blended learning is the practice of combining face-to-face instruction with online learning experiences. Many school districts are encouraging teachers to incorporate blended learning techniques into the traditional classroom model, in an effort to provide students with a more diverse educational experience. No longer are your students limited to learning only what you know or what the textbook says; rather, they have a limitless amount of information at their fingertips. Thus, the goal of teaching should be not only to impart content, but also to assist students in effectively seeking it out for themselves. In the blended learning model, the teacher acts as a facilitator who guides students as they access new information to ensure it is done in a safe, responsible, and purposeful manner.

As we consider ways to meaningfully incorporate technology in our classrooms, there is no better place to begin than Google Apps for Education. You undoubtedly already have a handle on what it means "to Google." After all, the company's powerful search engine is the most popular in the world. However, Google has also developed a sophisticated suite of productivity tools and made them available, free of charge, to schools around the globe.

From Gmail (Google's popular email service) to a host of other products like Google Docs (a word processing program), Google Calendar (an electronic scheduling and calendar solution), and Google Drive (a cloud storage service), Google's suite of communication-driven tools allow teachers and students alike to work smarter. Collaboration is king when it comes to Google Apps for Education. No longer do meaningful learning experiences have to be bound by the four walls of your classroom. Using Google Apps for Education, students can work collaboratively with you and each other and access information any time from any device.

For K–12 educators, the built-in creativity, productivity, and communication tools, increased efficiency, and cost-saving capabilities offered by Google Apps for Education provide an incredible opportunity to meet digital natives where they are and prepare them for life in the modern world. There is no single tool in the Google Apps for Education suite that is better suited to meeting educational needs than Google Classroom.

Google Classroom, at its most basic level, is an app that helps teachers easily and efficiently assign, collect, and return work to students. Of course, you could simply replace these once-analog processes with their digital counterparts, but truly harnessing the power of Google Classroom creates an opportunity to do much more. Classroom can serve as the foundation of your blended learning integration strategy. Google refers to Classroom as "mission control" for your classes; used purposefully, it can be the touchstone for all of the online learning your students will do throughout the year.

You likely already have a system in place to accomplish the tasks of assigning and returning work to students, so why replace that system with Google Classroom? Sure, it can streamline your work-flow process, but utilizing Classroom can also enhance your ability to communicate with students, differentiate instruction, and share new concepts and tools in real time. Embedded in the fabric of Google Classroom are new ideas and approaches to education. The focus on a partnership between students and teachers, the tools to access and disseminate valuable information in real time, and the ability to evaluate student progress and give instantaneous feedback make Classroom a game changer.

Aside from these larger implications, Classroom can also impact simple tasks and minor issues by helping to prevent them from becoming major headaches.

Imagine receiving this email:

To: Ms. Brock

From: Frustrated Parent

Re: Sam's Essay

Dear Ms. Brock,

Sam told me he turned his essay in on time and you docked him 10% for it being "late." Can you explain this?

Thanks,

Frustrated Parent

You've probably received an email or phone message resembling this one—an annoyed parent pointing out a discrepancy with the grade you've given and the one they believe their child has earned. This can be a source of irritation for both teachers and parents. But now imagine being able to simply respond with this:

Dear Frustrated Parent,

Attached you will find a time-stamped screenshot showing when Sam uploaded his assignment; it was submitted at 9:17 p.m. on Thursday night—unfortunately, it was due Monday morning. I understand Sam has a lot going on, but if he's unsure about due dates in the future, our class syllabus and calendar can be accessed 24/7 via our Google Classroom. Please let me know if you have further questions!

Ms. Brock

Or imagine receiving this note:

Ms. Brock,

I was out sick Monday, Tuesday, and Wednesday. What did I miss?

Stephanie

These types of requests can be exasperating for a teacher. Consider the time it takes to stop what you're doing and look back through lesson plans and calendars to figure out exactly what a student missed, not to mention the time required to gather the necessary resources for make-up work. Now, multiply that by the number of absences in your class every year. Think of how much time it could save you to be able to respond like this:

Stephanie,

All lessons, readings, and assignments are posted on our Google Classroom. Scroll down to locate the dates you were absent and complete the work as indicated. Email me if you need any clarification. Hope you're feeling better!

Ms. Brock

Google Classroom may not be the cure for every common teaching headache, but the paper trail it leaves behind can be invaluable. Think of the hundreds of times you have had to stop what you were doing and look back at old paperwork to solve problems or retrieve information for individual students.

So, who can use Google Classroom? Many mistakenly believe it is limited to middle and high school students, but it has a place in elementary schools as well. Truly, if your students can master the art of logging in, they can use Classroom. As with all educational tools, modification is key. Start slow and figure out how to best use Classroom with your students. A first grade teacher may simply post a link to a primary-friendly online spelling game. A third grade teacher may post a question and ask students to answer it, and then ask them to respond to one another's comments. A high school teacher may use Classroom as an exclusive portal for collecting and grading assignments. No matter how you put Google Classroom to work, it has applications at every level of education. The sooner students learn how to operate competently in the digital realm, the better.

The Benefits of Google Classroom

There are many advantages to using Google Classroom, but let's talk about some of the most beneficial reasons you should make the leap sooner rather than later. Google Classroom helps you:

GO PAPERLESS. At some point in your career, you have probably been encouraged by an administrator to use less paper, and rightly so. Paper, ink, and toner are costly consumables that school districts must constantly replace. The costs associated with purchasing and maintaining copy machines can quickly eat away at thinly stretched budgets. In addition, using large quantities of paper has environmental consequences. Google touts the paperless nature of Classroom's work-flow as one of its primary advantages. Think about how much paper is wasted in your class each year, and consider whether or not it's a necessary or thoughtful use of those resources. Taking your classroom digital means using less paper, which is good for everyone.

REDUCE STUDENT ORGANIZATION PROBLEMS. Using Google Classroom means both in-progress and completed work are in a single place. We've all seen it before: a bewildered and frustrated student rifling through an unkempt backpack or locker, desperately trying to find a missing page of homework. Utilizing Google Classroom means students always know where to find their work. Everything is automatically stored in a file on Google Drive. With easy-to-use search options and intuitive folder organization, it's rare for something to get lost. The student's work is safely tucked away as soon as it's created. In addition, since Google tools automatically save with every keystroke and provide a revision history, they make it nearly impossible to accidentally delete something. Everything is right there in the cloud.

...AND TEACHER ORGANIZATION PROBLEMS. Disorganization isn't exclusive to students; teachers can lose things, too! Sure, there are those who might have a perfectly maintained color-coded filing system, but most teachers have a few chinks in their organizational armor. Keeping track of late work and make-up work is enough to throw even the most organized teachers for a loop. Using Google Classroom, you can set clear due dates and have an up-to-the-minute record of everything that has been turned in. Plus, Classroom automatically stores everything in Google Drive, so copies of every original assignment and all student work are kept in Google Drive folders. If anything goes wrong, it's a simple process to go back, find the problem, and make it right.

EVALUATE BETTER. Because a copy of student work is saved in Google Drive, teachers effectively have a built-in system for storing everything a student does throughout the term. This system can be used in a variety of creative ways. At the end of the year, you could help students select their best work for a portfolio. Or, you might share a few projects from a student's file with curious parents at a conference. A student with an IEP or specific learning goals can have a clear record of work from which you and other educational professionals evaluate progress. These files may prove invaluable when determining new educational goals or implementing instructional scaffolding, a process based on tailoring learning to each student's needs and goals. There is no end to the potential uses of an on-demand record of every student's work.

TALK MORE. Google Classroom allows for a constant two-way stream of communication between students and teachers. You can use the Classroom stream to post announcements on which students can comment, or pose questions for them to answer. Even students who were absent from school can get in on a discussion. There is an opportunity to leave remarks and send comments to students at nearly every phase of the work-flow process. As most teachers know, leaving lengthy comments on student work done on paper takes time and often results in some serious hand-cramping, but utilizing the communication features in Google Classroom is far less time-consuming (and completely cramp-free). Much of student communication in their private lives is done electronically, so they are adept at communicating in this manner and appreciative when you take the time to send a digital note or comment. It doesn't have to be in red ink to mean something.

For these reasons, and so many more, Google Classroom can be a game changer for an educator. The innumerable ways the doors to our physical classrooms can be opened 24/7 via this digital portal can make a significant impact on the student learning process. The increased opportunities for communication with students can positively impact accountability and engagement. In addition, utilizing technology tools in the classroom offers students experiential learning in this new domain.

It is critical for today's students to become literate in responsible technology use. Already, students manage many of their relationships online, and as we've seen, this has resulted in too many making irreversible, life-changing missteps. Bringing technology into the classroom, modeling its responsible use, and facilitating students as they utilize it in real-world scenarios will provide them with the experience and know-how they need to avoid online fiascoes in the future.

Of course, Google Classroom should not be the sole mode of interaction with students. No matter how sophisticated a tool Classroom may be, it is still just a tool. Technology cannot replace meaningful student-teacher relationships, but with commitment and ingenuity it has the potential to make those relationships even stronger.

PART II

A Step-By-Step Guide to Using Google Classroom

Logging In and Creating a Class

Before we get started learning how to use Google Classroom, there are a few pieces of background information you need to know. Google Classroom is only accessible to students and staff of schools enrolled in the Google Apps for Education (GAFE) program. If you are unsure whether or not your school has a GAFE account, contact your technology director or support personnel for confirmation.

Your school's GAFE administrator has access to a dashboard where all users are assigned either a student or teacher role in Google Classroom. Teachers are able to create classes, whereas students are only allowed to join them (unless given a special designation by the dashboard administrator).

To log in:

1. Go to www.classroom.google.com.

2. Log in with your school credentials (i.e., the same username and password you use to access your email account).

3. The first time logging in, you will be asked to identify whether you are a teacher or student. It is very important that you clarify your status as a teacher at this step. If you inadvertently select "Student" and find that you are unable to create a class in Google Classroom, contact your GAFE administrator to correct your status in the administrator dashboard.

If you're new to any of the other Google Apps for Education, like Gmail, Google Docs, or Google Drive, you'll want to familiarize yourself with them. These applications work together with Classroom to create a seamless communication and work-flow process. Google Classroom depends on Gmail for communication, Docs for content creation, and Drive for storage, so it's important that you get acquainted with all three. If you've never used any of these apps before, do not panic.

A helpful tip for new users is to associate the Google Apps for Education tools with more familiar counterparts. For example, think of Google Docs as a counterpart to Microsoft Word. Google Docs is a word processing program just like Microsoft Word—with the addition of built-in communication tools that increase its functionality for teachers. Gmail is an email program similar to Outlook, Yahoo!, and other email systems you've likely used in the past. Google Drive is similar to the hard drive on your computer (or you could even say it's like a filing cabinet!), except instead of keeping your files locally, Drive stores them in the cloud.

Storing something in "the cloud" simply means that instead of storing it yourself by saving it to your desktop or a flash drive, you're enlisting the help of a cloud storage service and its servers to store it on your behalf. There are several examples of cloud services in addition to Google, such as iCloud and Dropbox. Once it's stored on their servers, you can retrieve your data through a web browser or app from any device, anywhere, anytime. While many cloud storage services cost money, Google offers GAFE users unlimited storage space for free.

Later, we'll talk more about how the other Google Apps for Education interact with Google Classroom to create a streamlined, paperless assignment flow between you and your students. For now, you've logged into Google Classroom and identified yourself as a teacher, so next we'll create a class.

Creating a class in Google Classroom is as easy as clicking a button. In fact, that really is all you have to do—click a button! In the top-right corner of your Google Classroom home screen, next to your email address, you'll see a plus sign icon. Click here and two options will appear: "Join class" and "Create class." Click the "Create" option, and you've done it! You've created your first Google Classroom just like that.

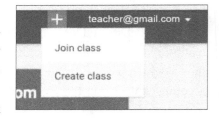

Now, let's go make it yours!

Taking the Google Classroom Dime Tour

You'll be taken into your Google Classroom as soon as it's created. It will look bare-bones at first, but don't worry; soon, it will be fully customized and ready to populate with content for your students. As you enter your Classroom, you'll see a message that reads, "Welcome to your class! Do you want to take a tour to learn more?" Clicking the "Start Tour" button launches a Google Classroom dime tour, so to speak. We'll help you follow along:

1. When you start the tour, it will highlight the plus sign icon in the bottom right of your screen. This button allows you to add announcements, create assignments, reuse old posts, and ask questions to the class.

2. Next, the tour will draw your attention to the Class Code. Your unique Class Code is like a secret knock for entering your Classroom. Simply share the number and letter code with your students so that they may join your Classroom. We'll discuss the Class Code in detail later on, but for now it's important to know that it is case-sensitive, meaning your students must enter the code *exactly* as it appears in order to be admitted to your classroom.

3. Now, the "Students" tab in the menu bar near the top of the page will be highlighted. Clicking on this tab will take you to the "Student" page. Here you will be able to invite students to your Classroom by email and manage student activity once they have joined your class.

With that, the tour is over. You're probably thinking, "*That's it*?!" Remember, it's just the dime tour! The brevity of this introductory tour, however, does highlight the best thing that Google Classroom has to offer: simplicity. Let's dive a little deeper into the different areas of your new Google Classroom.

Customizing Your Classroom

Many teachers spend their summers carefully selecting décor and laboring over bulletin boards to improve the look and feel of their classroom. After all, it's well documented that inviting, personalized spaces help students feel more comfortable and prepared to learn. For the same reason, you'll want to take some time to personalize your Google Classroom. Giving Google Classroom some of your unique flair reminds students that this virtual space is deeply intertwined with your physical classroom, and that the same rules and expectations apply.

There are two options for customizing the look of your Classroom. In the bottom right corner of the header image, you will see two buttons: "Select theme" and "Upload photo."

Selecting a Theme

Choosing "Select theme" will initiate a pop-up window with two tabs: "Gallery" and "Patterns." The gallery offers a bank of pre-selected images. Browse these to find an image that pairs well with your discipline—a band director might choose sheet music, a horticulture teacher may want a close-up of a leaf, or an art teacher may select a bright photo of colored pencils. There are lots of images to choose from, and they address a variety of content areas, as well as more general education themes (such as a brain!). If you select the "Patterns" tab, you'll be offered a selection of geometric and whimsical patterns in a variety of colors.

Whether choosing an image or pattern, simply click on the one that you want. A check mark will appear in the upper-left corner of the thumbnail you've selected. Click the "Select class theme" button at the bottom of the window to make the image or pattern you've selected become the header image.

Uploading a Photo

By choosing "Upload photo," you will be able to add a custom photo or image to the header. You might make the header image a shot of your desk or a picture of your students to connect the virtual classroom with the physical one. If your physical classroom has a theme, like Ms. V's Superhero Students, consider extending it to your virtual classroom. The header image can be changed at any time, so you can even regularly update it to reflect each new unit of study. If your students are members of multiple Google Classrooms, this personalization tactic will also help remind them of which class they have entered in the virtual realm.

Once you've uploaded or selected an image for your Classroom, it will appear in the header. You will have the option to change this going forward, so if you can't decide just yet, choose a placeholder and revisit it later.

The About Tab

Below the header image you've chosen, there is a solid-colored menu with three items: "Stream," "Students," and "About." Let's focus on the "About" section first. Once you click on the "About" tab, you will be taken to a page that allows you to enter information and upload files about the course and class. This step is optional, but adding more information up front will reduce the amount of questions you receive later.

Adding Class Details

The first blank is reserved for the title of the class. Try to be specific here; instead of entering just "English," try using "Ms. Brock's English Class" or "Sophomore Honors English." The next line offers an opportunity to describe the class in more detail. Here, you might write a brief overview of class objectives or just a few descriptive lines about the overall goals of the course. The next line, labeled "Room," asks, "Where does the class meet?" In this space, in addition to entering your room number, consider adding the days and times your class meets (i.e., Blue Days, 2nd Period or M–W–F from 8:00 a.m. to 9:00 a.m., etc.)

Accessing the Classroom Drive Folder

You will also see a line that reads, "Google Drive Folder," along with a folder icon and the title of your class. Google Classroom automatically generates this Google Drive folder to store all assignments and student work added to your Classroom. It's like having a filing cabinet that fills itself! Clicking the folder icon opens Google Drive in a new window, where you'll see that the folder is currently empty. Don't worry; it will fill up fast when you start adding content! We will discuss how to use the Google Drive folder later, but for now there's one very important thing to know: DO NOT DELETE THE FOLDER. Deleting the folder will cause you a lot of headaches later on, so it's important to leave it be for now.

Accessing the Classroom Calendars

Both an in-app Classroom calendar and a Google Calendar are created when you make your Google Classroom. As you add assignments and questions with due dates to your Google Classroom, those dates will automatically appear on these two calendars. You can access both of these calendars from the "About" tab.

View in Classroom

In the "Calendar" section of the "About" page, the first option reads: "View in Classroom." Clicking this link will take you to a weekly calendar within in the Classroom app that displays upcoming due dates. This calendar will automatically populate each time you add a due date to your Classroom to help both teachers and students keep track of upcoming assignments.

Open in Google Calendar

The second option, "Open in Google Calendar," links to Google Calendar, a separate Google application. If you're a Google Calendar (calendar.google.com) user, you will have noticed that Google automatically adds a calendar for each of the Google Classrooms you teach and are enrolled in as a student. This calendar is automatically populated based on the due dates assigned in Google Classroom. If a time is specified within a due date, the assignment will show up at that particular time in your Google Calendar. If no time is specified, it will show up as an all-day event on the due date.

You can also add custom events like guest speakers or field trips to your individual Classroom calendars. These are automatically added to your students' Google calendars as well. Just like any other Google Calendar, you may share your Classroom calendar with any other Google user. This includes those outside of your educational organization. You can also make the calendar public or embed it into your teaching website in order to share assignment due dates and upcoming events with parents.

Adding Course Documents

Underneath the box with all your class details, you'll see another box labeled "Add materials..." This is the perfect place to add course documents like a syllabus or list of class rules. If you have a form that your students will use routinely throughout the year, such as a reading log or observation sheet, you may want to add that as well. This is also a great place to add a link to your school or class website, or any other websites your students will use throughout the year. Don't bog this area down with assignments. Keep it limited to class documents that are pertinent throughout the duration of the term.

To add a document or other file, click the "Add Materials..." box, give it a title, and attach the material using one of the four icons.

Choose an icon:

- The paper clip allows you to upload all types of files (such as Word docs, Powerpoint presentations, Adobe pdfs, etc.) from your computer's hard drive.

- The Google Drive icon (the one that looks similar to a recycling sign) uploads documents from your Google Drive folders.

- The YouTube icon (the dark square with the light triangle) will allow you to link to a YouTube video.

- The chain link icon will link to any website. Just type in the site's URL.

Adding a Co-Teacher

To the left of your class information is a sidebar that features a picture of you (if you have one associated with your Google account), identifies you as the teacher, and includes a link to your email address. You'll also see an option to "Invite Teacher." When you click this, you'll see a pop-up window that shows your school contacts. Search or scroll to find the teacher you would like to add from the list. If you have a co-teacher, team teacher, or any colleague with whom you are otherwise collaborating, you can add them here so they may post announcements, add assignments, and assess student work.

A student teacher, mentor teacher, or administrator may also be interested in joining your Classroom in an observation capacity. In this case, you can add them as you would a student, which we will go over in the next section.

That's it! Once you've completed the "About" section, you'll have covered the five W's—who, what, when, where, and why—of your class. The benefits of having a fully-formed "About" page include:

- Students always have access to your contact information.

- Class objectives are clearly stated.

- There is no confusion about the date, time, or meeting place of the class.

- The syllabus and other important course information are accessible to students twenty-four hours a day.

You can always revisit this page and change course information as necessary.

Students Tab: Adding and Managing Students

Now that you've filled in all the general information about the class, it's time to populate your Google Classroom with students. Make sure your Classroom's theme and information are organized so that you are prepared for students to enter. You wouldn't want students walking into a disheveled room on the first day of school, and the same logic should apply to your virtual Classroom. Make all necessary preparations before inviting students in. When you're ready, click on the "Students" tab in the menu and you will be taken to a page that looks like this:

You'll note this page is relatively empty at first, but will soon hold the roster of all the students enrolled in the class. A message in the center of the page reads, "Invite students or give them this code to join," followed by the unique class code you were automatically assigned when you created the class.

Students can gain entrance to a class in one of two ways. "Invite" students to join the Classroom via email or direct them verbally to classroom.google.com and give them the class code. First let's discuss how to invite students to your class via email.

Inviting Students to Classroom via Email

By clicking the blue "Invite" button on the Students page, you will initiate a pop-up window with your school contacts. It is important to remember that you may only invite people to your class who share your school domain or who are from a trusted domain (see your GAFE administrator to find out if your school has any trusted domain partners). Your school's domain name is how Google recognizes you and the other members of your organization. For example, if your school email address is teacher@sampleschool.com, your domain is sampleschool.com, and all of your students must share that domain name in order to be admitted to your Google Classroom.

For the most part, this system provides excellent access for students and privacy for your online learning community. However it can sometimes be problematic. If you work for a special education cooperative that services several school districts, for example, you may work with students with email addresses of varying domains. Some school districts even assign separate domains for teachers and students. If this is an issue for you, contact your district's Google Apps for Education administrator about whitelisting trusted domains. Whitelisting enables people in different domains to interact using Google Apps for Education, but can only be initiated through the GAFE administrator console.

From the window, choose the students you wish to invite. You can do this by scrolling through the list of contacts or by typing the student name or email address in the search bar located in the top-right corner. When you see the name of the student you'd like to add, simply click the box to the left of his or her name to check it. Once the name is checked, it will be added to a list at the bottom of the window. Once you've checked all the students you'd like to invite, click the "Invite Students" blue button. This will send a mass invitation to each of the students you've selected to join your Google Classroom.

INVITING STUDENTS BY EMAIL GROUP. You also have the option to invite a preset email group. If you have a group email set up, you can click the "Group" tab at the top of the window and check the box next to the desired group. Click the "Invite Students" button, and an email will be sent to each member of the group, inviting them to your Google Classroom.

The email sent to students will provide them with your name, the class title, and a clickable link that will lead them directly to your Google Classroom.

Once you have invited students, their names will appear in a list on the Students tab. If a student has not yet accepted the invitation to join, the name will be greyed out and a note reading "Invited" will appear to the left. Clicking the envelope icon next to any student name will initiate another email to the student. Once your student accepts their invitations, their names will no longer be greyed out, and you will have successfully added them to your Google Classroom.

Using the Class Code to Join a Class

Your other option is to share the unique class code with your students. You could email it to them or write it on your board the first day of class. In order to join the class using the class code, students will first have to go to classroom.google.com and sign in with their school email address and password.

NOTE: If a student is having difficulty signing in, it may be because they are already signed into Google with a personal Gmail address. If that is the case, have them log out and log back in with their school email address. If this does not solve the problem, contact your school's Google Apps for Education administrator, who will be able to pinpoint what's wrong on the administrative dashboard.

After students have successfully signed into Google Classroom, they must click the plus sign in the top-right corner of the page and choose "Join Class." A pop-up will appear asking the student to enter the class code. It should be entered exactly as it appears on your "Students" tab. Once the student enters the class code, he or she will click the "Join" button to be taken to the Google Classroom with which the code is associated.

Choosing Student Settings

Back on the "Students" tab, you'll see students beginning to populate your Google Classroom. As they join, the "Invited" notation will disappear, and they will officially become a student of your Classroom. In the Student View of your Google Classroom, the "Students" tab is labeled "Classmates." When students click on the "Classmates" tab, they see the names of all their peers enrolled in the class, as well as the email icon. Clicking on this icon allows them to easily communicate with their classmates.

For teachers, the "Students" tab is not just for inviting students to the Google Classroom, it is also the key to student management within the app. A drop-down menu reading "Students can post and comment" appears at the top of the "Students" page. Clicking this button will reveal three options for student posting and commenting permissions in your Google Classroom.

Students can post and comment

"Posting" refers to your students' ability to share messages and content on the Google Classroom Stream, while "commenting" refers to their ability to respond to posts put up by you or another student. The default setting is "Students can post and comment," which means that students can freely post messages and reply to and comment on others' posts. If you allow students the ability to post, they will see a plus sign in the bottom right corner of the page when viewing the class stream.

 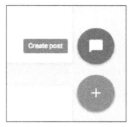

Clicking the word bubble icon brings up a box in which each student can write a post to share with the class. Notice the four attachment options—the paper clip, Google Drive, YouTube, and chain link icons—in the box. These allow students the ability to not only post thoughts, questions, and ideas, but also to share multimedia content.

Allowing students to post and comment increases the communication function of Google Classroom. Picture a panicked student posting this announcement the night before a big test: "Help! Can someone explain the checks and balances system to me again? I'm so confused!" Teachers and fellow students would be able to answer the student's call for help, and provide them with information when they need it most. A twenty-four-hour service like Google Classroom means that questions no longer have to wait until tomorrow, or, worse yet, go unanswered altogether.

In this capacity, your Classroom can be its own little social networking site. With the benefits of constant communication, however, come the drawbacks. If you choose to provide your students with these communication tools, it is important to also set expectations and guidelines for using them.

Students can only comment

The second option, "Students can only comment," gives students permission to reply to or comment on things you have posted, but not to initiate messages or content posting. Allowing students to comment but not post is a great way to encourage discussion while still controlling the Classroom's content. Think of how many times you have seen people contribute diverse opinions to an interesting Facebook status. Posting a food-for-thought item, such as a video clip or provocative question, and asking students to comment on it is a great way to initiate discussion on a topic you are introducing in class. By the same token, we've all seen conversations like this go awry. Perhaps an argument breaks out, or an incident of cyberbullying or inappropriateness takes place. As the teacher, you have the ability to delete any posts or comments added by a student.

Only Teachers Can Post or Comment

The final option, "Only teacher can post or comment," eliminates student posting and commenting altogether. If this setting suits your needs, then by all means choose it. Keep in mind, however, that allowing students the opportunity to contribute to the conversation has the potential to strengthen both student-to-teacher and student-to-student communication, as well as overall student engagement.

Resetting Your Classroom Code

You'll notice that your class code is also visible on the "Students" tab, along with a drop-down menu consisting of two items: "Reset" and "Disable." You may want to reset your class code for a variety of reasons. Perhaps it has a zero, and you're afraid students will confuse it with a capital O. Maybe

you're concerned an unauthorized user has attempted to join using the code. Whatever the reason, you can reset the class code as many times as necessary. You can also disable the code altogether and so restrict student entry to invitation-only.

Actions

The final function on the "Student" page is the "Actions" menu. Clicking this menu gives you three options: "Remove," "Email," and "Mute."

- REMOVE: Click the checkbox next to a student name(or multiple names) on your roster and then the "Remove" button. This completely removes the student(s) from the class. Use this when a student has joined your class in error or dropped your class. If you remove students by accident, don't worry. You can always invite them again!

- EMAIL: Click the checkbox next to a student name (or multiple names) on your roster and then the "Email" button to initiate an email to the student(s).

- MUTE: Click the checkbox next to a student name (or multiple names) on your roster and then the "Mute" button to eliminate a particular student's ability to post and comment. If you have a problem with only a few students making inappropriate comments, you may consider using this option rather than eliminating commenting and/or posting for the entire class.

Now that you know how to add and manage students in your Google Classroom, it's time to start adding content.

The Stream

By default, when you log in to a course you've created in Google Classroom, you will arrive at its "Stream." This is the communication hub of your class. Here, you will post assignments, announcements, and questions for your students. If you've granted them permission, the Stream is also the place where student posts and comments will appear. Before you begin to fill your Stream with content, let's take a look its different components.

The Layout

UPCOMING ASSIGNMENTS. Let's begin by examining the left-hand sidebar. The first box, or widget, reads "No work due soon." When you begin, this box will show no upcoming assignments, but as you add assignments with due dates, you will see them listed here in the order of nearest due date. When there are no assignments or the assignments are due more than a week in the future, the box will read "No work due soon" as it does now. In Student View, it may read slightly more enthusiastically: "Woohoo, no work due soon!"

DELETED ITEMS. Below the upcoming assignments, you'll see a box labeled "Stream" with a toggle to "Show deleted Items." If you would like to view items you've already deleted in addition to items currently on the stream, click this to toggle it to the "on" position. Viewing deleted items will also show you any items that students have posted and deleted. Students do not have the ability to see any deleted items.

CLASS CODE. Below the deleted items box, you can see another "Class Code" box indicating the code needed to join the class. The Class Code appears in many places so that you and other users are ready to provide it whenever necessary. Because it is, in essence, the key to the Classroom, it is important to have it handy at all times.

TOUR. Moving right to the larger main column, you can still see that offer to go on a tour of your Classroom. As you start posting, this option will disappear and you will simply see the content you've added to the stream.

ADD ICON. In the bottom right corner, you will see the plus sign icon. Here, you will input questions, assignments, and announcements for your students. We'll talk more about these important functions in a bit, but for now know that you will be adding all content utilizing this icon.

Clicking the plus icon brings up a menu of four items: "Reuse post," "Create question," "Create assignment," and "Create announcement." Simply click the icon associated with your desired choice to initiate that action.

THE QUESTION MARK ICON

Looking away from the "add" icon and its menu, you'll note a small question mark in the lower-left corner of the screen. When you click the question mark, you are given a menu with four options: "What's New," "Send Feedback," "Ask a Question," and "Get Help."

- WHAT'S NEW. This links to a page on Google's support site listing the new features they've added to Classroom. Check here often, as new features are being added all the time, especially in these early stages.

- SEND FEEDBACK. This option allows you to initiate a message to Google. Google encourages its users to send feedback regarding problems or issues, share ideas for new features that would enhance the product, and offer general reviews about experiences with the app. Teachers and students should take advantage of this feature, as Google is known to improve its products and add new features based on user feedback.

- ASK A QUESTION. This links to the Google products forum, where you can pose questions that forum moderators and other Google Classroom users may answer. This method of crowdsourcing for solutions is a quick way to find out how other students and teachers are using Google Classroom and how they solve problems to which you cannot find solutions elsewhere.

- GET HELP. The final item on the question mark icon's menu directs you to the Google Classroom Help Center, where you can receive help troubleshooting any problems you may encounter with Classroom. There are sections for "Teachers," "Students," and "Administrators" of Google Classroom. Simply click on the area in which you require more information and follow the prompts to locate what you're looking for. Bear in mind that the Help Center will offer you only prewritten, step-by-step instructions on how to use different features of Classroom. You may need to talk to one of your school's more experienced users or your Google Apps for Education administrator if you require additional assistance.

Now that you've familiarized yourself with the Stream page, it's time to start posting.

Posting an Announcement

Posting an announcement in Google Classroom is easy. Simply click on the plus sign in the lower-right corner and then the "Create announcement" word bubble icon to bring up the announcement window. Before you start

announcing news to your students, let's learn about the announcement's purpose, posting instructions, and potential uses.

An announcement is a message that you send out to your students. Unlike an assignment, an announcement asks students to only look at it, rather than respond with some sort of work. Announcements can be messages, videos, webpages, or other pieces of content. Below each posted announcement, there is a space for you and your students (depending on the student permissions you've established) to add comments.

Adding Content to Announcements

You have several options for creating an announcement. You may just want to post a text-only message, such as the one in the photo below. In this example, a teacher has posted a text-only announcement to remind students to turn in permission slips for an upcoming field trip.

Alternatively, you may want to deliver some sort of material using the announcement attachment tools. There are four different options for attaching content to an announcement.

UPLOADING COMPUTER FILES. Clicking the paper clip icon brings up a window that allows you to attach files from your computer. Simply drag the files you'd like to upload onto the window or click "Select files from your computer" to choose files from your hard drive, external drive, flash drive, etc. to upload to your Google Classroom. At the top of this window, there are two other tabs, "My Drive" and "Starred," which link to files kept in your Google Drive folders. Starred files are files that you have indicated are important by starring them.

ATTACHING GOOGLE DRIVE FILES. The Google Drive icon attaches items from your Google Drive files. Clicking it brings up an identical window to the one the paper clip icon initiates, but this time it defaults to the "My Drive" tab instead of the "Upload" tab. Thus, by clicking on the correct tab, you can easily use either icon to search both your Google Drive and hard drive folders.

ADDING YOUTUBE VIDEOS. The YouTube icon allows you to link to a video from YouTube to your stream. Clicking the icon produces a window that allows you two options.

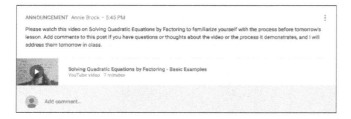

- VIDEO SEARCH. You can search YouTube directly from this tab by using keywords. For example, if you were teaching students how to solve quadratic equations by factoring and wanted them to watch a few examples of the process before your lesson, you could use the "Video Search" function to find appropriate examples by typing in the key words "quadratic equations factoring." Search results will always be listed in order of popularity based on your keywords, just as they are when searching directly on the YouTube site. Be sure to watch a video in its entirety before posting it to your Google Classroom to ensure that it is appropriate for your students and relevant to your purpose.

- URL. If you already know which video you'd like to post and so do not need to utilize the search function, simply click on the "URL" tab and paste in the video's web address.

After using either method to select a video, click the "Add" button. Prepare a message to go along with the video and click "Post" to share it with the class.

ADDING WEB LINKS. The final option for attaching content to an announcement is by adding a link. Click the chain link icon and type or paste the URL of the page you'd like your students to visit. You might want them to check out a site to review concepts or read an article. Remember, if you want a due date attached to whatever you're posting, you'll need to use the Assignment function. If it's simply information you want students to consume, however, you can post it as an announcement.

Cross-Posting an Announcement

As you are adding announcements to your Classroom stream, you should be aware of a few more tools you can use.

Whenever you add an announcement, you'll see a drop-down menu that shows the name of the Classroom in which you are posting. Clicking this drop-down menu brings up a checklist of all the classes you've created in Google Classroom. If you are making an announcement you'd like to post in more than one of your classes, simply add a checkmark next to each of the Classrooms in which you'd like the message to appear. This will cross-post the announcement to each of the specified Classrooms. This function will save you from having to enter the same announcement multiple times.

Editing and Deleting Announcements

The two final features of the announcement function appear after you have already posted your message. There is a column of three dots in the top-right corner of each posted announcement. Click here to edit or delete the announcement you've created. Once you've made the necessary edits, click "Save" to update the post.

Posting an Assignment

The Assignments icon is, as they say, where the magic happens. The most significant benefits of Google Classroom are evident in the utilization of this function. Once teachers initiate the assignment flow process, it can be done from start to finish completely paperless. The "assignment flow" process refers to the various stages in the life of an assignment. Broken down into steps, assignment flow looks like this:

1. Teacher creates assignment.

2. Student opens and completes assignment.

3. Student turns in assignment.

4. Teacher grades assignment and returns with comments.

5. Repeat as necessary.

With Google Classroom, teachers can remain in constant contact with the student throughout the entire work-flow process.

Google Classroom works most effectively when combined with the other Google Apps for Education. Consider having students write assignments in Google Docs and create presentations in Google Slides instead of using Word or PowerPoint. Utilizing these programs allows you to look in on the progress of student papers and projects and offer feedback before the final due date.

Typically teachers create an assignment and don't see it again until it is turned in for grading. Using Google Apps for Education, both teachers and students can have access to assignments from the very beginning. As a teacher, you can access a document remotely while the student is working and make suggestions and offer feedback in real time. This is far more relevant than a few red-ink comments given weeks after an assignment has been turned in.

Not all of your assignments will be created using Google Docs or other Google Apps for Education, but incorporating those programs into the Google Classroom process will significantly increase its functionality and usefulness.

Creating an Assignment

So how do you create an assignment? Assignments are similar to announcements; click the plus sign and then choose the "create assignment" icon to initiate the assignment window. In this window, you will provide details about the assignment. Remember—the more information you provide up front, the less questions you'll have to answer later.

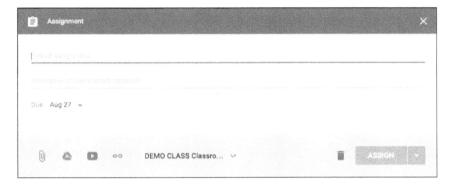

NAMING YOUR ASSIGNMENTS

When creating an assignment, you'll be asked to give it a title. Creating a consistent naming convention for your assignments is strongly encouraged because for every assignment created in Google Classroom, a folder of the same name is created in Google Drive. The students' finished assignments are kept in these folders. If there is a discrepancy with a grade or whether or not something was turned in, or if you simply want to access a past assignment for assessment purposes, you'll want to be able to locate it quickly and easily.

Bearing in mind that whatever you name your assignment at this point will be the name it is given in your Google Drive archives, it is important to create a logical naming system. Alice Keeler, who provides Google Classroom tips and tricks on her blog, alicekeeler.com, recommends using a numerical system (i.e., Biology.001 or #001 Biology). You may also consider organizing by unit and type of assignment (i.e., Assignment 1.1 would be the first assignment in Unit 1 and Quiz 2.3 the third quiz in Unit 2). No matter what naming convention you concoct, it should be easy to remember for both you and your students in order to retrieve assignments as efficiently as possible.

Each student also has an automatically-created Google Classroom file in his or her Google Drive folder. Each time you create an assignment, a folder of the same name will appear in their file as well. In this way, each student will have a record of the work they have done throughout the year. This intuitive filing system can prove invaluable when it comes to evaluation and assessment of learning outcomes.

Adding a description

After naming your assignment, your next task is to describe it. In this area, you can include the instructions, expectations, goals, etc. of the assignment. If you have a rubric, you may want to include that as an attachment since assignment posts can have multiple attachments.

Specifying a due date

Next, you are asked to provide a due date for the assignment. This date is important because it will be included in reminders to students and utilized in organizing the "Upcoming Assignments" widget next to both student and teacher streams. You may add a specific time that the assignment is due; otherwise, the assignment will be considered late if it is not turned in by 11:59 p.m. of the due date indicated.

You also have the option to not include a due date at all. You may use this feature when providing optional extra credit opportunities, or in any other scenario in which a due date is unnecessary. Simply toggle the "Due date & time" switch to the off position.

Attaching files

Now that you have filled out details regarding the assignment, you'll want to attach any necessary content to complete the assignment. Attach content the same way as you would with an announcement (page 21). Simply click on the correct icon to upload files, attach files from Google Drive, link to a YouTube video, or include a web link. Remember that you may attach more than one piece of content. For example, in a single assignment post a teacher might upload a rubric from his or her computer, add a Google Slides template for a presentation, and include a link to a website that explains how to correctly cite academic sources. Attach as much as you think is necessary for your students to successfully get the job done.

Editing permissions

The final step before posting your assignment is to adjust viewing and editing permissions on any Google Drive document you've attached. Let's imagine you want students to fill out a short questionnaire you've created in Google Docs as an introductory activity for the beginning of the year. In a drop-down menu next to the Google Docs file you have attached, there are three options: "Students can view file," "Students can edit file," and "Make a copy for each student."

STUDENTS CAN VIEW FILE. Choosing this option allows students to open the document but not change it in any way. In other words, they can look but not touch.

STUDENTS CAN EDIT FILE. This allows students to add to, change, and delete content on the document you've attached. This option is helpful if you are conducting a group brainstorming activity or selecting time slots for presentations. All students can make their mark on a single shared document.

MAKE A COPY FOR EACH STUDENT. This final option is most appropriate for the sample activity above. When you indicate the "Make a copy for each student" option, Google will generate a unique document for each student using his or her name when the student opens the file. So the file you've named "Assignment.001—Student Introduction" when opened by your student Lila Smith will become "Assignment.001—Student Introduction—Lila Smith."

This is an excellent option to use when you are providing a document or worksheet to be filled out by the students.

Otherwise, you may simply provide the instructions to the assignment, and the students will create their own documents, presentations, or projects from directly in Google Classroom or upload work at a later time.

Publishing an Assignment

When you are ready to post an assignment you've created, simply click the blue "Assign" button. Notice the down arrow on the blue "Assign" button; when clicked, it will give you the option to save your assignment as a draft. Click the "Save draft" option if you are not finished with creating the assignment or do not want to post it yet. The draft, along with any others you've saved, will remain at the top of your stream until you're prepared to publish it.

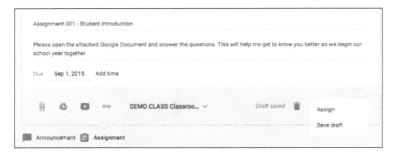

After you publish an assignment, it will appear in the Classroom stream much like an announcement, but with a few differences. You'll have the option to make comments on assignments, as will students if you've elected to give them that permission. But you'll also see the addition of some key information. Looking at an assignment in the stream in Teacher View, you will see the due date and time for the assignment (in this example, Sep 1, 11:59 p.m.), as well as a running count of how many students in the class have completed it.

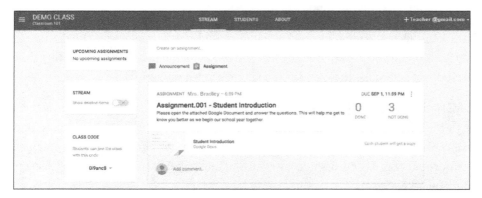

When clicked, the three vertical dots next to the due date bring up a menu of options: "Move to top," "Edit," and "Delete."

MOVE TO TOP. Clicking this option bumps a post to the top of the Class stream. You might use this function to help students easily locate an announcement posted far in the past that has been buried under new items. If you notice that several students have yet to turn in an upcoming project, you can move that assignment to the top of the stream as a reminder for students to keep on top of it.

EDIT. This option allows you to make changes and corrections to a post.

DELETE. This option removes a post completely from your stream. If you delete an assignment, any associated attachments will remain in the Google Drive folder.

Assignments in Student View

Students viewing an assignment in their own streams have an area to add comments to the post, assuming you have given them that permission. If students fail to turn in work by an assignment's due date, they will see a red "Late" notice in the top-right corner of the assignment's post. There is also an "Open" button in the top-right corner of these posts; clicking it takes students to a page that includes any instructions and/or attachments you've provided.

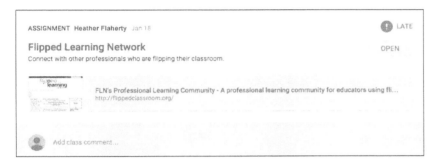

Below the assignment's details, there is a box titled, "Your work." In this area, students will know whether or not the assignment is past due by the presence of the red "Late!" text in the upper-right corner. Google Classroom generates this warning when students fail to mark assignments as done before the due date indicated.

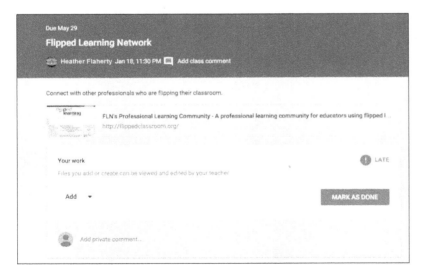

Completing an assignment

Students have several options for turning in assignments. Clicking the "Add" button displays a menu with two sections: "Add" and "Create."

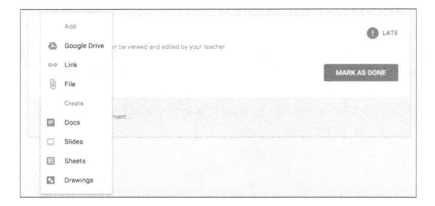

ADD. This choice provides students the ability to pick a file from their Google Drives, post a link from the web, or upload a file from their electronic devices (students using the Classroom iPad app will have the option to upload items from their camera roll). Students can initiate content creation directly from the assignment page in Google Classroom as well.

CREATE. Under the "Create" header is a set of options for creating content utilizing different Google Apps. This includes Docs for writing essays and other word processing tasks, Slides for creating presentations, Sheets for developing spreadsheets, and Drawings for rendering diagrams, charts, and other design-based tasks. Any content created using these tools are automatically posted on the assignment and shared with the teacher from the moment they are created. This means that if a student fails to click the "Mark as Done" button to indicate they have finished an assignment, a teacher can still go into the student's file to evaluate whatever work has been completed.

BEING PART OF THE PROCESS

In Student View there is a message that reads, "Files you add or create can be viewed and edited by your teacher." Again, this means that you as a teacher can access student content from the assignment screen the moment it is added or created. Students should be encouraged to use this function as soon as they begin an assignment, as it allows you to be part of the creation process from the beginning. This gives you an opportunity to access student work and offer guidance and feedback every step of the way.

Turning in an assignment

It is up to the students to turn in the required work by clicking the "Mark as Done" button to indicate they have completed the assignment. Once the "Mark as Done" button is clicked and the assignment is turned in, the assignment can still be unsubmitted by the student to make changes. However, if the assignment is re-submitted after the due date, it will be marked as late even if the student initially submitted the assignment before the due date.

Either way, once something has been uploaded or attached to the assignment by the student, the "Mark as Done" button turns to a blue "Turn in" button. The distinction between the two is the "Mark as Done" indicates that a student has completed an assignment task, but it did not require them to upload or attach any digital content (i.e., "Read chapter two" or "Construct a suspension bridge model using cardboard and string.") Whereas the "Turn in" button indicates that the student is going to turn in a piece of digital content as part of the assignment.

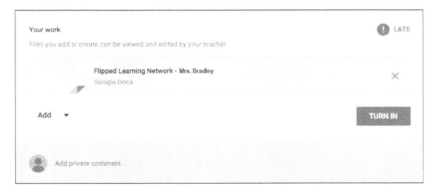

Once a student clicks the "Turn in" button, they will be greeted with a window asking them if they are sure they'd like to turn in the work. This second-chance screen gives students the opportunity to change their minds before they turn in the assignment. Once the student confirms they would like to submit the assignment, the assignment page changes to include an "Unsubmit" option.

"Unsubmitting" an assignment

In Student View, students can unsubmit previously turned in work to make changes. Again, if the work is unsubmitted prior to the due date and subsequently re-submitted after the due date, the student's work will be considered late by the system. A student will know whether or not a finished assignment was turned in late by the presence of a green indicator in the top-right corner of the assignment page. If the work was completed on time, there will be a green check mark along with the word "done." If the work was turned in late, it will read "done late."

These clear time stamps and late indicators can alleviate many classroom issues, since they make it nearly impossible for teachers to lose track of submitted assignments or for students to engage in deceptive practices.

The Assignment Page

Returning to the Teacher View of Google Classroom, you will see that clicking on any assignment title in your stream brings you to a page dedicated to that single assignment.

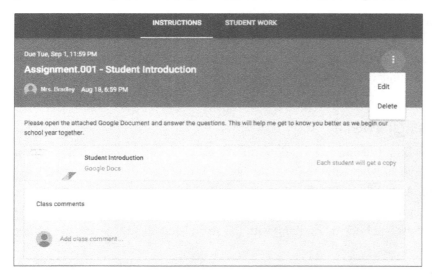

First, notice the solid menu bar at the very top of the page. On its left side is a back arrow that can take you back to the Stream. In its center are two tabs: "Instructions" and "Student Work."

The "Instructions" tab displays information about the assignment, including its title and the details you provided when you initially posted it. The due date, class comments, and any attachments are also displayed. This view shows you essentially all the information available to students through the class stream.

The "Student Work" tab is more complex and so will need further elaboration.

Student Work

The "Student Work" tab includes information only you can see. Its menu, which appears immediately below the assignment page menu, provides a "Return" button to give the graded assignment back to students and a drop-down menu to assign it a point value.

Downloading Student Grades

At the far right of the Student Work menu bar is a gear icon that, when clicked, offers you the opportunity to download student grades for this particular assignment or student grades for all assignments. All data will be downloaded as a .csv file that you can use to transfer grades from Google Classroom to your electronic grade book where compatible.

Viewing the Roster

In the left sidebar of this page, there is a roster of students enrolled in the class. The roster is divided into two sections: "Done" and "Not done." This area is where you will indicate the grade each student receives on the assignment and write private comments for students about their work. Clicking the name of a student on the roster causes the main area of the screen to show details of that particular student's assignment.

Choosing Assignment Icons

Below the menus, the name of the assignment appears at the top of the page in large, bold text. Below this are rows of square icons, one for each student enrolled in the class, indicating whether the assignment has been completed or remains unfinished. These icons, in addition to a running tally at the top of the web page, show teachers visually whether or not students have turned in their work. For example, the figure at the top of this page shows that one of the three students in the Class has turned in the assignment. Clicking the arrow next to the "All" button displays a drop-down menu to allow the teacher to view icons for all students, only those who have completed the assignment, or only those who have not yet done it.

Displaying Individual Assignments

To view a specific student's work, click either the student's name in the left side bar or the student's icon in the main area of the screen. To evaluate an assignment, click on the student's attachment(s) and they will automatically open in a new browser tab. Once you've looked over the work, simply close that tab to automatically return to your Google Classroom tab. If the assignment was created with a Google application, there is no need to worry about saving as you add comments. Google apps automatically save after every keystroke, so your comments will not be lost even if your computer crashes.

Grading Assignments

At this point, you'll be ready to grade the assignment. In the "Points" drop-down list in the Student Work menu, you can indicate the point value an assignment is worth. You may choose one of the pre-selected point values Google offers, including 1, 20, 50, and 100, or you can enter a different point value by typing it into the box or indicating that you'd like the assignment to be ungraded.

Once you've completed this step, you can enter student grades. Click on "Add Grade" next to a student's name on the roster in the left-hand sidebar. In the example pictured, the student earned 18 points out of 20. Here you also have the opportunity to offer feedback by way of adding a private comment. Simply type the feedback in the "Add private comment…" box and click "Post." Once you have posted a private comment, you can click on the three dots on its right side to edit or delete it.

Viewing Submission Histories

An additional feature on the student's assignment page is the ability to view the student's submission history for this assignment. Click "See submission history" under the student's name at the top of the page. This allows you to see when the student submitted and/or un-submitted the assignment and how many times this was done before the due date.

Returning Assignments

When you're done with grading and commenting, simply click the "Return" button at the top-left of the screen to give back to students their graded work. Any students with a check mark next to their names will receive their grades and comments. In order to do a bulk return so that all students receive their graded assignments simultaneously, wait until you have graded every student's work and then click all the blank boxes to fill them with check marks. All selected students will have their work returned to them.

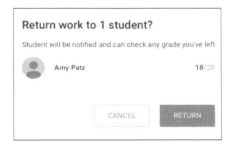

After returning student work, a pop-up window will remind you that each student will automatically receive an email indicating that you have graded the assignment. They will be allowed to view their scores and your comments at this time.

Changing Grades

Classroom allows you to change the grade of assignments after your original assessment.

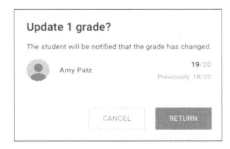

This is a fantastic feature, particularly if the student needs another opportunity to successfully complete the assignment and demonstrate mastery. The process is exactly the same as it is for first entering a grade, and you even have the chance to add new comments. Simply "Return" when you've made the necessary changes. Students will be alerted to any changes in their assignment grades via email notification.

THE CLASSROOM WORK-FLOW ADVANTAGE

There you have it. This process of assigning, grading, and returning is known as the assignment flow. It may seem that this is a time-consuming process, but once the steps are learned it goes very quickly, especially when you consider all the tasks that the assignment flow is replacing.

Before digital tools like Google Classroom, you would go to the copy machine to make copies of the assignment for each student. Then, you would pass out the copies, dictate instructions, and answer any student questions. The student would then take the assignment home, and, if it wasn't misplaced or otherwise forgotten, he or she would finish it and physically hand it in on the due date. After students physically handed in the assignment, you would collect the papers, take them home, grade them, record the grade in the grade book, take the assignments back to school, and deliver them to each student with handwritten comments and feedback.

Google Classroom removes almost all the potential for error and frustration in the assignment flow. Assignments are stored in the virtual world, not to be lost in the cluttered bottom of a backpack. Reminders are consistently sent and displayed so that students are always aware of due dates, and teachers receive clear notifications when those due dates are not met. Teachers no longer have to spend time fixing paper jams in the copy machine or lugging home workbooks to be graded by hand.

In addition to solving for many of the missteps that can happen in the process of assigning student work, Google Classroom also offers many opportunities for communication and clarification on assignments. Not to mention, utilizing Google Classroom creates a digital record of the work a student has completed throughout the year, helping schools assess and evaluate long-term student progress.

The best feature of Google Classroom's assignment flow, however, is that a teacher can pop in at any point in the process to offer guidance and feedback. The lines of communication are open from the time the assignment is initiated to the moment it is turned in—and beyond!

Asking a Question

Returning to the stream, there are still more ways to use Google Classroom. Clicking the bottom right plus icon and choosing "Create question" from its menu displays a new window through which you can pose questions to the class.

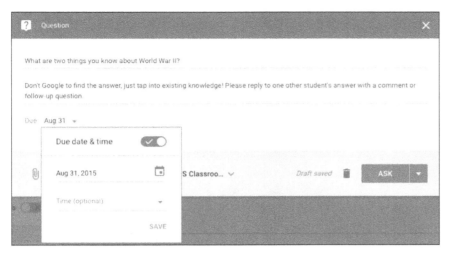

Posting a question to the Classroom stream is a great way to start a discussion, take a poll, or conduct a quick formative assessment. You can use this feature to spark question-driven discussions or do a quick check for understanding in order to help engage students. In the example shown in the figure above, a teacher is checking for existing knowledge before starting a unit on World War II.

The question feature is very similar to the assignment feature. When creating a question post, you can attach supplementary computer documents, Google Drive files, YouTube videos, and web links. Simply type in the question you'd like to ask and add any pertinent details and additional materials. Questions, like assignments, are accompanied by due dates and can be graded in the exact same manner. Clicking the due date area reveals a menu in which you can specify the date and time when an answer is due. Once your details are sorted and you're ready to ask the question, just click "Ask." You can also save a draft of a question just like you can save assignment drafts.

Setting Commenting Parameters

Before posting the question, Classroom will ask you how students are allowed to interact with it. By clicking to put check marks in the boxes, you can determine whether or not to allow students to see and reply to each other's answers or to edit their own answers. Typically when allowing students to reply to their peers' responses, you may want to prevent them from editing their initial answers. If a student changes an answer after it has been commented on or replied to, this could potentially make for a confusing exchange.

Grading Questions

As already stated, questions are graded in the same way as assignments. Assign a point value (or choose "Ungraded"), grade the student's answer, and then return the work. Just like you can comment on assignments, you can add comments to returned student answers.

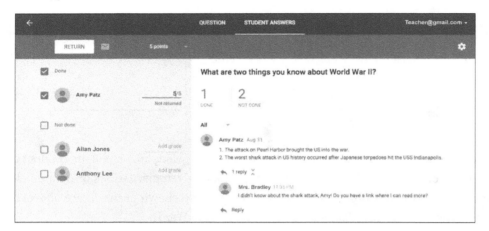

Reusing Posts

The "Reuse Post" option allows teachers to reuse announcements, assignments, or questions from any of their classes, past or current.

The final option on the plus sign menu at the bottom right of the stream is "Reuse post." Clicking this option will open a window that lists all the classes you have created. Click on the class that houses the post you'd like to reuse. This will bring up another window with a list of all the posts ever added to the class you selected.

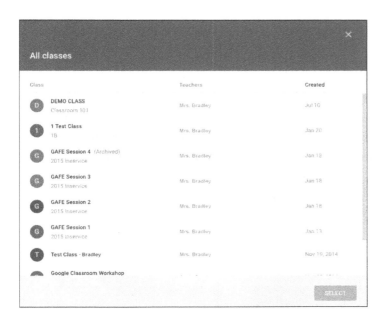

Clicking on the post you'd like to reuse will highlight it. At the bottom of the window, check the box if you want to create new copies of all the attachments associated with that post for this Classroom's Google Drive folder. Then click "Reuse" to display a new window with details of the post. You may now make any edits, add new attachments, or otherwise change the old post to customize it for your current class. After making these changes, simply assign or post it as you do with all other announcements, assignments, and questions.

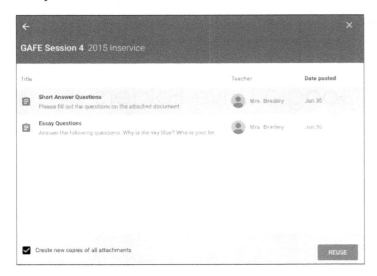

The Home Screen

Click the "hamburger button"—the square icon with three parallel horizontal lines in the top-left corner of the screen (it kind of looks like a hamburger, doesn't it?)—in the top-right corner and choose the house icon to go back to your home screen. Here there are icons for each of the classes you have created on your Google Classroom account, as well as any classes you have joined as a student or co-teacher. The home screens of students show icons for each class in which they are enrolled.

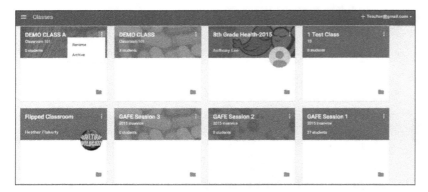

Renaming or Archiving Classes

In each box on the home screen, you'll see the title of a class you have created or in which you are enrolled. For any class you have created, you can click the three vertical dots in the upper-right corner of its box. This gives you a drop-down menu that allows you to either rename or archive the class.

Accessing Classes' Google Drive Folders

One easy way to access the Google Drive folder of any of your classes is to click the small folder icon, which you can see in the bottom right corner of every class box on your home screen. Clicking this icon takes you directly to the Google Drive folder associated with this class.

Accessing Assignment Lists

Clicking the hamburger button will display a drop-down menu with two lists: one of classes you have created and the other of classes you have joined. At the top of each list is a clipboard icon and the word "Assignments."

Assignment To-Do Lists for Students

In Student View, clicking on this clipboard icon leads to a new window from which students can choose to view either a chronological list of assignments they have completed or a list of assignments they have yet to do. This feature is excellent for helping students stay on top of deadlines and prioritize work. A student who struggles with organization or procrastination might make a habit of checking the not-yet-done list several times a day to be reminded of upcoming assignments.

Assignment To-Review Lists for Teachers

When you click on the clipboard icon as a teacher, you will be shown a new window that has two viewing options: "To Review" and "Reviewed."

- TO REVIEW. This viewing option displays a list of the assignments you've created that have turned-in student work not yet evaluated or graded.

- REVIEWED. This viewing options displays a list of your assignments for which you've evaluated and graded all turned-in student work.

These lists can help teachers get a quick visual handle on their incoming workload and on the class progress toward an assignment's completion.

Changing Your Settings

Click the "hamburger button" and scroll to the bottom to reveal a "settings" icon (a grey cog). Clicking this brings you to a page that can help you manage the settings for your Google account, and for your Classroom in particular.

Google Account Settings

When it comes to your Google account, you have two options.

CHANGE PROFILE PICTURE. You can upload an image from your computer or use any image on your Google Drive as your profile picture.

GOOGLE ACCOUNT SETTINGS. Clicking this lets you fine-tune the settings currently applied to your overall Google account profile. These settings include, among others, updating your password and adding secondary contact information like a cell phone number.

Google Classroom Notification Settings

Also on the Settings page is a section titled "Notifications," which allows the user to check or un-check a box labeled, "Send email notifications." By default, Google Classroom notifications will be turned on. It is highly recommended that students keep them turned on so that reminders of upcoming due dates and teacher feedback can be delivered directly to their email inboxes. If students are using the mobile version of Google Classroom with either an Android or iOS device, they will also have the opportunity to enable mobile notifications. If enabled, these push notifications will appear on their electronic device whenever a student or teacher responds to their posts, mentions them in a comment, or sends them a direct message.

Enabling or disabling notifications is a personal preference. Many social networks offer notifications when someone tags you, mentions you, or posts something to your wall. Receiving too many messages becomes annoying and cumbersome to sift through.

A student may check Google Classroom often enough to not need notifications to be reminded of assignments to complete and questions to answer. Some students prefer to check each of their Classroom courses at specific times of the day when they can immediately address any new developments. Other students may want notifications to keep them apprised of updates and messages from the teacher.

Accessing the Classroom Calendar from the Home Menu

As we saw in the "About" section, Google Classroom generates an individual in-app calendar for each class, but you can also access a master calendar that displays due dates for all of your classes. To view the master calendar, click the "hamburger button" at the top-left of the Classroom home screen. The second option on the resulting drop-down menu is "Calendar." When you choose this option, you'll be taken to a color-coded calendar that shows what assignments are due when in your various Classrooms. You will automatically start on the current week, but you can use the arrows at the top of the page to navigate to different weeks. Clicking a colored assignment block on the calendar will take you to a page that shows data and details associated with that assignment. In Student View, when a student clicks on a colored block, they will be taken straight to a page where they can turn in the assignment. There is a drop-down menu labeled "All Classes" at the top-left corner of the calendar displaying all your classes that allows you to toggle from the master calendar to the calendar of a specific class.

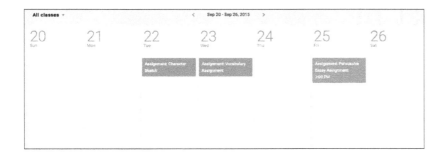

Tips and Recommendations for Classroom Users

As you read this step-by-step guide for operating Google Classroom, remember that Google is adding features all the time, some of which may not be addressed here. If you're unfamiliar with a new feature, just play around with it! It's important to remember that everything you do in Classroom can be undone. If you post something by mistake, you can delete it. If you delete something by mistake, you can retrieve it. Trial and error is key to becoming an experienced Classroom user.

Here are a few final tips and recommendations for using Google Classroom:

- Download and use the Chrome browser to get access to apps and add-ons that can optimize your Google Apps for Education experience.

- Though images in this guide are from the desktop version of Classroom, there are also app-based versions for tablets and smart phones available in the Google Play and Apple App Stores. They look very similar to what you've seen here.

- Classroom is available in forty-four languages. Google Apps should default to the language specified in the user's account. Make changes as necessary.

- Follow the students' lead. Sometimes kids can be quicker with technology than grown-ups. Encourage your students to discover different ways to use Classroom, and then put their ideas into practice.

- Ask for help! If you are struggling in some area of Google Classroom, seek advice from other users. Whether your appeal is made to your GAFE administrator, a fellow educator, or directly to Google forums or staff via the question mark icon, there will be someone who has faced your particular issue and can help you determine the next steps.

PART III

Practical Applications of Google Classroom

Now that you're familiar with the various features and functions of Google Classroom, how can you make the most of it? Once you've created a Classroom for your students, it's important to update it regularly, in order to encourage students to check it each day. The more you use Classroom, the easier it will be operate its various features and pick up on the new ones constantly being released. In this section, you'll find tips and tricks for maximizing the benefits of Google Classroom, as well as ideas for classroom applications.

PROFESSIONAL DEVELOPMENT. Google Classroom is an excellent tool for all sorts of learning, including professional development for teachers. Digital professional development is gaining popularity as teachers are able to interact with a professional network and learn new skills and concepts when it's convenient for them. Encourage teachers in your district to create Google Classrooms to share their expertise and insights. One teacher might create a Classroom with modules teaching an effective behavior management plan. Another might create a Classroom to demonstrate a new instructional method. These "teach the teacher" opportunities are endless with Google Classroom. An added bonus? Teachers are able to see Google Classroom through the student's lens. Because there are two different interfaces for teacher and student, it's imperative the teacher becomes familiar with what students are seeing.

TEAMING. Google Classroom can also serve as a long-term communication tool for teaming. Teachers in a particular grade, team, group, or committee might use the Classroom tools to conduct conversations on tier groups, specific student needs, or curriculum. The assignment function can be used when teachers need to turn in a report or submit a lesson plan; the question function can be used to initiate a conversation on curriculum or student needs; and the announcement feature can be used to share resources, plan field trips, and coordinate events. The communication options, privacy considerations, and built-in reminders, make Classroom an optimal tool for use in teacher groups.

CURRICULUM IMPROVEMENT. Gaps and redundancies can exist in even the most well-developed curriculum plans. Consider utilizing Google Classroom as a way to identify and mitigate these issues. For example, a teacher may notice that students are not yet proficient in a skill they should have mastered the year before, and present evidence from student work in Google Classroom to the curriculum director to help close the gap. Or it may come to the attention of an administrator, who has joined Classrooms in an observatory role, that two teachers are teaching the same novel. Identifying and sharing this kind of critical information gleaned from Google Classroom, along with student work as evidence of the knowledge or skills gap, can help shore up any weak areas of the curriculum.

OBSERVATION STATION. Ask a teacher in your discipline to add you to their Google Classroom so you can see what kinds of things are happening in another class. The act of observing a teacher as they interact with students can be an invaluable learning tool. This could be especially helpful in a mentoring relationship, so that a first-year or student teacher could observe a veteran teacher in action.

UP YOUR EVALUATION GAME. Google Classroom can be an extremely useful tool for administrators. Though it would be nice to spend lots of time sitting in on classes and observing teachers and students, that's not always possible. Joining the Google Classrooms of teaching staff as a student can allow an administrator to get a sense of what's happening in any class at any time. This bird's eye view can also help administrators make better informed evaluations. An administrator may even pinpoint examples of particularly innovative or effective lessons or projects, and ask teachers to present at a professional development event or otherwise share those tips and techniques with fellow teachers. Used appropriately and responsibly, this type of connectedness has the potential to improve the entire culture of a school.

BELL RINGERS. Use the "Ask a question" function to pose a question to the students at the beginning of class time, or post a link to a food-for-thought article or video and ask a question about it. Using the due date function, you can make these questions due in the first ten minutes of class so that students will know to get to work on them right away. If students have time after they post an answer, they could comment on other student answers. This type of open-ended discussion can be a great way to initiate student engagement early in the lesson.

CLUBS AND STUDENT GROUPS. Teachers and school personnel can use Google Classroom to share information and coordinate with students in clubs and athletic teams. A football coach could use it to post game film for student athletes to review or post diagrams for them to study before a big game. A chess club instructor could share a link to an article on strategy or an online chess game. The possibilities are endless! If you have a need to share and communicate with students, you can put Google Classroom to work for you.

STUDENT PORTFOLIOS. Content students create in Google Classroom is kept in a folder on their Google Drive, which means they are keeping a running record of everything they've done throughout the year. This means a student using Google Classroom essentially has a built-in portfolio of their work. Using these "portfolios," teachers can have students select their best work to send home or showcase, share work with other education professionals, or evaluate progress students have made over the course of the term.

PHOTO DOCUMENTATION. Teachers often assign projects that are not digitally driven, but even then Google Classroom can be used to virtually showcase that work. An art teacher might have students photograph sculptures they are creating and upload those images to be displayed, commented on, or used for instructional purposes. An English teacher might ask students to hand-draw a map of a novel's setting or sketch a character, and then photograph or scan and upload these images so that they become part of their students' digital portfolios. Lessons involving manipulatives and hands-on activities do not necessarily negate the need for Google Classroom. It's still a great way to display work and get feedback.

GET THE "SHARE TO CLASSROOM" EXTENSION. The "Share to Classroom" Chrome extension allows teachers to automatically share content they find on the web with students. When both a teacher and his or her students have the extension on their devices (which can be added individually or for everyone by a GAFE administrator), the teacher can go to any website, click the "Share to Classroom" button, and like magic, the website pops up on all student devices. This extension prevents you from having to painstakingly dictate long, cumbersome URLs to students. It's also very useful if you want to show students something on the fly. Let's say in the middle of a geography lesson, a student asks where the Nile River empties. The teacher can quickly pull up a map online, click the "Share to Classroom" button, and just like that all students in the class can see on their devices a map of the Nile emptying into the Mediterranean Sea. To find the extension, go to the Chrome store and search for "Share to Classroom."

UPLOAD WORKSHEETS. Yes, you can still use pre-made worksheets. Simply scan the worksheet or document you'd like students to fill out and post it to your Classroom. Using the Google Drawing tool, for example, students can create text boxes to fill in the blanks or use the shape tools to draw diagrams. This is a great way to save paper!

GET STUDENT FEEDBACK. Encourage students to utilize the comment stream that comes with each announcement and assignment to ask questions and provide feedback. If students are continually asking the same question or don't understand a directive for a particular assignment, this can signify that a change to your directions is necessary. This feedback can help you tweak and revise assignments to avoid problems and confusion in the future.

YEAR-END REFLECTION. Reflection is a major buzzword in education, and for good reason. Teachers should review lessons and units often and with a critical eye in order to continue to provide the best learning experiences for their students. At the end of the school year, however, it's sometimes difficult to look back over the entirety of the year to consider changes to the overall structure and flow of the class. But with Google Classroom, teachers have a running record of what went on every day of class. In reviewing the stream, teachers have the opportunity to examine what worked and what didn't, and can make changes to improve the overall impact of the course.

ATTACH A GOOGLE FORM. Though this feature has not yet been implemented at the time of publishing this manual, Classroom will soon allow teachers to add a Google Form directly to a post (currently you can add only the link to a Google Form). In Google Forms, you can create surveys, quizzes, and tests, and responses are automatically organized in a spreadsheet for easy grading. Using Google Forms is a simple way to conduct formative assessments quickly and easily. To try out Google Forms, go to forms.google.com.

TALK, TALK, TALK! From bulk emailing to direct messages, interacting with students has never been easier. There is no shortage of opportunities for teachers to leave comments, notes, feedback, and questions for students. What makes Google Classroom stand out among similar online classroom management tools is its emphasis on communication and ease of sharing information. Take advantage of these opportunities to up your communication game and keep your students engaged in classwork outside of designated class times. Gone are the days of tracking kids down in the halls or trying to find a good time to meet with a student to clear up a small issue. The tools embedded in Google Classroom allow you to simply exchange a quick message with a student to clear up a misunderstanding or refocus a student on the task at hand. Not only is Google Classroom simple and seamless, but it also, in relying on short electronic messages between teachers and students, employs a communication strategy with which most students are already very comfortable.

BEHAVIOR MANAGEMENT. Classroom comes equipped with tools to "Mute" disruptive students or delete their comments, but the messaging function is a great way to conduct behavior management before you have to resort to this option. Simply click the message icon to send a quick email to a student asking them to refocus. It's a great way to make discipline immediate and private without having to single out a student in front of the entire class.

KEEP KIDS SAFE. The ability to quickly view and attach YouTube videos from Google Classroom is a concern for some teachers. Along with immensely helpful and useful YouTube videos, there are some that may be deemed inappropriate for the classroom. Work with your school's Google administrator to use the restriction settings to limit the kinds of videos students can view.

TURN THE TABLES. Assign a different student each week to provide a thought-provoking article and discussion question for their peers to answer. Incorporating student-led instruction can help students "buy in" to a topic and feel ownership over their own education. Classroom makes it easy to provide opportunities for students to share their individual passions, which is an easy way to personalize the instruction to suit student interests and introduce the class (and the teacher!) to new ideas.

BUMP THOSE POSTS. The "Move to top" feature allows a teacher to move an assignment that has been driven down the stream back to the top. For example, if you assign a book project at the beginning of the term to be completed at the end of the term, you might want to bump the assignment post every few weeks to keep it fresh in the students' minds. When it comes to students, there is no such thing as too many reminders!

GIVE FEEDBACK TO GOOGLE. If you or your students would like to see new features added to Google Classroom, use the question mark icon to offer up new ideas. Google team members actually read this feedback, and many of the updates and new features that have been added to Classroom since its inception have come directly from user feedback like this.

WHOLE-CLASS ACTIVITIES. Set up a Google Slide template that students can edit and ask each student to research and create one slide on a given topic. Give the students a twenty-minute deadline for creating their slide and have each student share their slide. Bam! You have a class-created presentation made in twenty minutes or less. You can also employ this group-work strategy to brainstorming and note taking. Simply open a Google Doc with open editing privileges and have students start contributing!

KEEP CURRENT. Since its arrival, Google has added features and updates to Classroom on an almost monthly basis. Click the question mark icon and the What's New text to keep on top of these new features. Additionally, there are some wonderful Google Plus groups dedicated to discussing all things Classroom. Join one to see how other professionals are using Classroom across the globe. Or you can search #google-classroom or #gafe on Twitter to connect with other educators using Google Apps for Education.

FLIP YOUR CLASSROOM. A "flipped classroom" is one in which the instruction portion of a lesson is done as homework, and the homework portion of the lesson is done in the classroom. This allows the student to consume a lecture or watch examples outside of class time, in order to prepare for application of the concept during class time. This allows active work to be done under the guidance of the teacher. For many people, this model just makes sense; students usually have the most questions when they're in the process of solving a problem or writing an essay. Google Classroom makes this process of flipping a cinch, since you can easily upload video lectures and examples for students to watch and read. They can add any comments or questions these materials spark, and you can be prepared to dive into the lesson the next day.

IT'S FOR EVERYONE! Library media specialists, counselors, speech pathologists, gifted coordinators.... Any professional in the school setting can establish a Google Classroom. Even if a staff member doesn't work with students on a daily—or even monthly—basis, a Google Classroom is still a great tool to provide information to and keep in touch with students in the building. A counselor, for example, could set up a Classroom and add every student in the school in order to share anti-bullying or digital citizenship modules and resources. A library media specialist could do the same for academic research techniques or library procedure guidelines. If the goal is communicating with kids quickly and effectively, any education professional can make use of Google Classroom.

SAVE THE TREES. It goes without saying: The paperless nature of Google Classroom is among its most attractive features. Any school interested in saving money or environmental resources can do so with Google Classroom. Consider making a contest out of it. Get teachers trained and using Classroom, and then compare paper and copy costs from the prior year to see how much of a difference it can make. You might even have a statistics or economics class run the monthly numbers to show the ongoing financial impacts of reducing paper usage in school.

DIFFERENTIATION, REMEDIATION, AND ENRICHMENT. You can post both video tutorials for students who need additional instruction to master a skill or concept, or post follow-up activities for those who quickly achieve mastery and are hungry for more. Because there is no limit to how many attachments a post can have, a teacher can easily provide a variety of resources to suit different learning needs. There are a myriad of ways to use Classroom to increase differentiation in your instruction. For readings, post links to articles with different levels of text complexity. For projects, consider providing resources grouped by reading level and other measures for students with varying needs.

LOOK TO THE FUTURE. At the end of a course, a teacher can "archive" a class. When a teacher uses this archiving function, the Classroom is preserved as it was on the last day of the term. The teacher and the students involved in the class retain the ability to look at it anytime they like, though edits and changes cannot be made unless a teacher activates it again. Why is this important? A teacher may want to use past classes to help them construct new ones. A student may want to look back at an assignment or discussion for a refresher. There are any number of reasons a teacher or student might want to revisit a past class, and having the ability to do that is another reason Classroom is such an incredibly education-friendly product.

WRITER'S WORKSHOP. Consider conducting a writer's workshop using Google Classroom. Students simply post their written work, so that peers can offer positive praise and constructive criticism. Some students may feel self-conscious about sharing their work, but collaboration provides them with the necessary feedback to improve their writing. You wouldn't have the members of a basketball squad do all their practice individually; nor should you have the members of your class do their work in isolation. Publishing and workshopping writing can open your students' eyes to new ideas and ways of writing they hadn't considered before.

ACT/SAT PREP. Not all students have the time or money for college entrance exam tutoring. Start a Classroom dedicated to test prep. Posts could include a question of the day, links to tips and tricks, practice assessments, and more! You could even use the integrated calendar feature to schedule face-to-face study groups and guest lecturers.

PROJECT-BASED LEARNING. In project-based learning, students dive deep into a given question or problem by doing research and investigation over an extended period of time. Google Classroom is well-suited to project-based learning application because it allows teachers to curate resources and routinely check in on progress. Also, the various creation and content options give students choices in what information they share and how they do it. Because there are so many feedback and revision opportunities, students can continually submit and re-submit projects until they get it right. And, remember, not everything with a due date has to be graded. So, a teacher can assign a task associated with the ongoing project that has a deadline, but not necessarily a grade, attached. This allows both teachers and students to focus on developing skills rather than getting a grade.

SMALL-GROUP WORK. Google Classroom has the potential to enhance small group activities or learning centers, and keep a record of the work done during that activity. Simply post the procedure for each of the centers in the assignment directions, and attach the digital materials necessary to complete the task. Use the creation and commenting functions to make it truly interactive!

GUIDED EXPLORATION. Design a webquest and post a Google Doc with the tasks you'd like students to accomplish, as well as all the links to the sites they need to visit in search of information. Beyond webquests, Classroom can help anytime a teacher needs to curate a list of resources for students to access. All relevant links and documents can be attached to a single assignment or announcement so that students can find the resources they need quickly.

TAKE ADVANTAGE OF PRE-MADE TEMPLATES. Google has a template gallery that includes tons of fantastic resources for educators. There are graphic organizers, templates for games like Jeopardy, and other useful pre-made tools created by education professionals. The pre-made templates even come with starred reviews so you can read what other teachers thought of them and how they put them to work in their own Classrooms.

PARENT INVOLVEMENT. For very young students, send home the student login and password so that parents can help students log on to the Classroom at home. You can post videos and pictures from school events, showcase student work, and add links to resources to keep students engaged at home. You can also use the Classroom to share information about upcoming events or volunteer sign-up sheets with parents.

AVOID THE SUMMER CURSE. It's no secret that kids lose valuable information over the summer, but Google Classroom never stops working. Post summer reading challenges or links to DIY projects and activities students can do at home. You might even start discussions with incoming classes as a way to develop a rapport and start building relationships both with and among students before the school year begins.

SEMINAR ACCOUNTABILITY. If you manage a seminar or study hall in your room, create a Google Classroom for students who are assigned to you during this time. You may not be assigning work to them, but you can help students manage their time and stay accountable by requiring them to post a journal entry briefly outlining the work they completed that day or week. Students can also use Google Calendar functions to let the teacher know if they'll be absent from seminar for a meeting or event by indicating their whereabouts on a class calendar.

GO MOBILE. Google Classroom provides free, user-friendly apps in both the iOS and Android app stores. The desktop version has a few more features (especially where teachers are concerned), but students can easily complete assignments, respond to questions, and post content from their mobile devices. Encourage students to download the app as another way of staying on top of due dates and announcements.

There are so many more ways to put Google Classroom to work for you and your students. Take time to connect with other educators who are using Classroom in interesting and innovative ways. Check the Google Apps for Education blog or YouTube Channel often for tutorials and new features. There are several Google + communities dedicated to discussing best practices in using Google Classroom, and you can use other social media networks like Pinterest and Twitter to discover how teachers are using Classroom at their schools as well.

Best of luck as you seek to establish Google Classroom as "mission control" for your course work-flow. Remember, incorporating technology into the classroom isn't only a good idea because today's students find it interesting and engaging; it's important because tomorrow their livelihoods may depend on understanding how to use it effectively and appropriately. And, thanks to you, they will.

Acknowledgments

Thank you to all the wonderful people of USD 336 in Holton, Kansas, especially Amy Oldehoeft, Dr. Joe Kelly, Stacy Lasswell, Heather Hundley, Inga Nordstrom-Kelly, and Tom Sextro who provided support on this project. Thank you to Keith, Alice, and all the people involved in the production of this book. Thank you to Google for creating incredible educational tools like Google Classroom and making them available free of charge for teachers and students around the world. My deep appreciation to Jared, Bodhi, and Lila Brock for your endless love and support.

About the Author

Annie Brock is a freelance writer based in Holton, Kansas. She has worked as a high school language arts instructor and a middle and high school library media specialist. Annie is a Google Certified Educator, and does consulting on educational technology.

More books from Kingfisher Press:

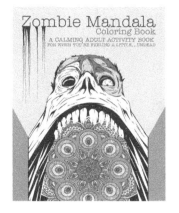

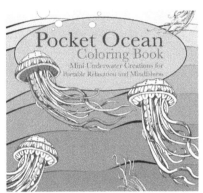

www.kingfisherpressbooks.com